Yaya's Journey to Assisted Living

Yaya's Journey to Assisted Living, provides the opportunity for a conversation about the aging process. It illustrates and expresses the stages of life. Joy, grief and letting go and why having a positive attitude about life's journey is important as we age. *Yaya's Journey to Assisted Living* is read by families, schools, and communities.

Inspiration for Yaya's Journey to Assisted Living

Over the years, I have moved aging seniors into assisted living communities. Most don't want to leave their homes. Who can blame them? Many have lived there for decades and have fond memories of a life past.

Then one day it was time for my mom to move to assisted living. She could not live alone. Like other seniors she did not want to leave her home. Finally, she realized with a fresh outlook on life everything works out for the best.

From my heart, I wrote this story about *Yaya's Journey to Assisted Living*.

A Special Thank You and Dedication

Yaya's Journey to Assisted Living is dedicated to all seniors and families who are faced with life-altering decisions. For my children and grandchildren, letting them know it's ok when it's time for Yaya to move into assisted living.

A special thank you to Mariann Romero, for the beautiful hand-drawn images, that bring the story to life. I am grateful for the friendship nurtured along the way. Together we created a story to help families who are moving their loved ones into assisted living.

Appreciation to David Reeser, Founder of Ojai Digital | Blue Jay Ink, graphic designer, author, photographer and teacher for fine tuning the book and a can-do attitude about all possibilities and options.

Thank you to Christine Weimer, author, poet, and editor for the exceptional editing suggestions, moving the story forward and checking in with supportive encouragement.

Yaya's Journey
to Assisted Living

by Mary Lynn Brook
illustrated by Mariann Romero

Yaya loved the color yellow. When she saw it, she smiled and her heart filled with joy. She loved it so much she painted her little house yellow.

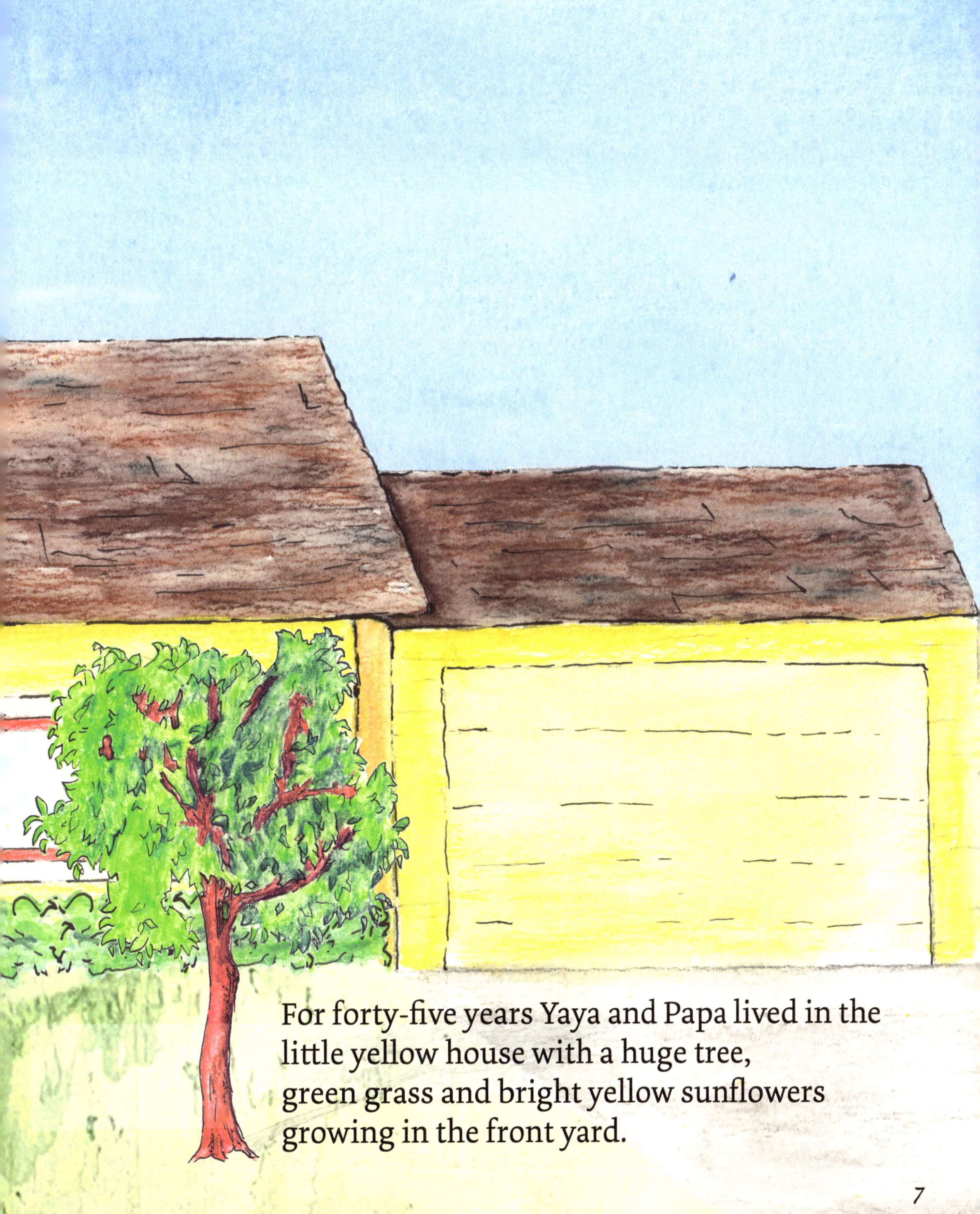

For forty-five years Yaya and Papa lived in the
little yellow house with a huge tree,
green grass and bright yellow sunflowers
growing in the front yard.

Mia, the playful family dog, watched the pretty yellow birds and chased the squirrels in the backyard.

When Yaya walked through the front door, Mia ran to meet her and gave her dog kisses. At night Yaya and Mia cuddled on the couch together. She was part of the family and went everywhere with Yaya and Papa.

The kitchen was the heart of the home. Yaya mixed her homemade banana bread in a big blue bowl and baked it in the oven. While the banana bread baked a warm comforting smell filled the house.

Papa clapped his hands together and declared, "That bread smells DELICIOUS, my mouth is watering and my stomach is growling. When will it be ready?"

Past the kitchen, down the hall was Yaya's little yellow bedroom. A beautiful blue and yellow cotton quilt lay across the bed. On the bedroom walls were pictures of Yaya's and Papa's children, Ken and Michala.

Below was a shelf with her favorite lifelong treasures.
An old wooden box filled with photos.

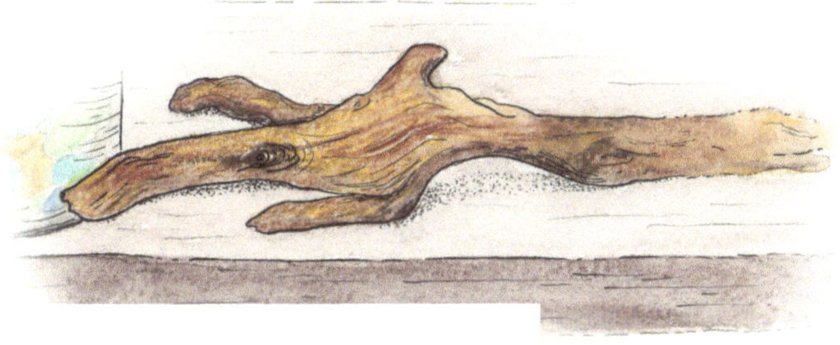

A piece of driftwood found on the beach.

A tall jar filled with seaglass.
When Yaya looked at her treasures, her mind would drift back to each adventure she shared with Papa.

Laughter and love filled the house as Michala and Ken grew up.

On hot summer nights when the fireflies started to glow, they would play hide and seek in the park across the street.

Time passed. Ken and Michala moved out of the little yellow house into their own homes.

Together Papa and Yaya aged in the little yellow house. Papa slowed down, sat in his chair and watched Mia play in the backyard.

One day, Papa went to heaven leaving Yaya and Mia alone in the little yellow house. Yaya was heartbroken. She sadly looked at Papa's empty chair day after day.

Then Mia grew old. She didn't chase the squirrels or watch the birds. She soon joined Papa in heaven. Yaya missed the cuddles on the couch and the dog kisses. It was lonely living in the little yellow house. She lost all her motivation and purpose in life.

Yaya no longer baked banana bread. She forgot to cook her meals or wash her clothes. The green grass turned brown and the yellow sunflowers died.

Ken and Michala worried about Yaya living alone. She could not keep her house clean and tidy. She did not leave the house or visit with her friends.

They thought in an assisted living community Yaya would spend time with her friends doing activities she enjoys. She could paint her room yellow and fill it with her life time of treasures and memories.

She would be around happy, cheerful people
who would take care of her.

A caregiver would help Yaya with her shower and help
her get dressed. They would make sure she took her
medication on time, wash her clothes, fold them, and
put them away. Caregivers would walk with her so she
would not lose her balance and fall.

When Michala and Ken spoke with Yaya they told her how wonderful it will be to live in assisted living. She could sit by the fountain and read a book or go to the movies with friends.

Yaya said firmly, "No, I am not moving to a new home. I love my little yellow house filled with all my memories."

"I'm afraid to let go of my treasures and try new things. I have lived in my little yellow house for many years. It's where we raised the children and Mia chased the squirrels."

Yaya worried all night about moving to assisted living.
She paced back and forth all night thinking about what
would happen to her as she grew older.

Yaya reflected on her choices carefully weighing her decision.

"Should I move to assisted living and leave my little yellow house?"

A peace and calm came over Yaya as she looked out
the window at the rising sun.

"I have lived a wonderful life in my little yellow house with Papa and Mia.

It is time to start something new. It will be fun to share little treasures and memories with my new friends."

Yaya called Ken and Michala to let them know the great news. "I am moving to a new home!" Yaya moved...........

At first, Yaya was nervous about being in a new home. But after a few days she settled into a daily rhythm and routine.

As she walked to the dining room, she admired the birds and butterflies in the garden.

She smiled to herself as she entered the dining
room. The comforting smell of freshly baked
cookies filled the air as her new friends welcomed
her to the table with a hot cup of tea.

After her tea, Yaya went to the activities room
anticipating a fun-filled
afternoon with her friends.

She painted with watercolors,
joined a singing class and was
the Queen of Bingo. Road trips
to museums and movies were
her favorite.

Later in the day, Michala and Ken came
for a visit. They found her reading her
favorite book in the garden surrounded
by flowers.

It made them happy to see Yaya living a
full and enriched life in her new home.

At the end of each day, Yaya reflects on her new life. She shares her old memories with her new friends and enjoys the activities.

She is comfortable in her little yellow room and the caregivers are friendly.

Yaya is at peace and glad she had the strength to move to assisted living.

Questions about loss, grief and moving on with a positive attitude.

Why was Yaya afraid to move to a new little yellow room?

How did Yaya feel when Papa and Mia went to heaven?

Why was Ken and Michala worried about Yaya?

What made Yaya change her mind about moving and leaving her home?

Was Yaya happy in her new community?

Mary Lynn Brook

Mary Brook, an expert in the Senior Industry, has helped seniors and their loved ones with the aging process for many years. She received her Bachelor of Arts degree in Communications from The Ohio State University. She currently holds certifications as a RCFE Administrator, Yoga and Personal Training.

Her experience as a Life Enrichment and Marketing Director, Director of Resident Care and Associate Executive Director in several RCFE facilities throughout the United States, gives her an unique in-depth perspective to helping seniors improve the quality of their lives.

She is the author of **Yaya's Journey to Assisted Living,** a children's story helping families reflect on the aging process of those they love. Mary currently works as an Associate Executive Director at an assisted living facility in Santa Barbara, California.

She and her husband hike, play soccer and live with their dog, Mia in Ojai, CA. They visit with their children and grandkids and enjoy new adventures.

Mariann Romero

A retired art teacher of 30 years, Mariann is now volunteering at the Santa Paula Art Museum Creativity Center, working with children and adults. Creatively, Mariann has embarked on new forms of art such as: wood working, gourds, and gel printing. Illustrating this book she described as, "...stepping out of my comfort zone, but the process was rewarding, and working with Mary was such a joy."

Outside of the art world Mariann enjoys nature through hiking, surfing and gardening.

She lives in Ventura with her husband, as their two children establish their own lives.

www.ingramcontent.com/pod-product-compliance
Lightning Source LLC
Chambersburg PA
CBHW041632110726
48005CB00002B/578